THE UNCOMMON MINISTER

VOLUME 5

D1153491

by

MIKE MURDOCK

TABLE OF CONTENTS

Unless otherwise indicated, all Scripture quotations are taken from the King James Version of the Bible.

The Uncommon Minister, Volume 5
Copyright © 1999 by Mike Murdock
ISBN 1-56394-104-X

Published by Wisdom International
P. O. Box 99 • Dallas, Texas 75221

To avoid the burdensome verbage of him/her; his, hers throughout this book, the simple reference to all of mankind, male or female, is simply "he" or "him."

❧ 1 ❧

Master One Topic In The Bible.

Know one subject more than anyone else does.

When I was 15 years old, an extraordinary minister came to my father's church. He was articulate, brilliant and persuasive. He took a special interest in me, and I responded.

"No man has the right to call himself a man of God who reads less than 20 chapters a day in the Scriptures," he declared. "Read the Scriptures daily, continuously. *Become an authority on at least one topic in the Bible.*"

I believed him. So, at the tender age of 15, I began to read the Bible consistently, a minimum of 20 chapters a day. Later, I began reading 40 chapters a day which helped me read the Bible completely through every 30 days. Some would criticize this method of reading a lot of Scripture thinking you could not retain very much. However, I discovered reading the Scriptures continuously brought an increased awareness of the passion of God, a relationship with His people. Rather than simply read three or four chapters a day that would "keep the conscience okay," I really wanted to have a general working knowledge of Scripture.

As I matured, I focused on one topic at a time. Now, I have discovered that your knowledge can soar quickly when you develop a passion and focus. Suppose you wanted to know everything in Scripture about *"Faith."* That's a marvelous subject. In fact, without *faith* you cannot even please or pleasure God. God has a desperate desire to be believed.

Here Are 10 Helpful Thoughts On Mastering One Topic In Scripture:

1. *Read Through The Bible And Circle In Red (Or Highlight In Pink) Every Scripture Relating To The Topic Of Faith.* When you open your Bible, you will immediately see every Scripture connected to your focus, *Faith.* Mark those Scriptures that reveal the benefits and blessings of *using* your Faith. This will include *examples* such as Joshua and Caleb in the Old Testament. Highlight Scriptures that show the consequences of *not* using your *Faith.* Your goal is to become an authority on *Faith.*

2. *Create A Yearly Calendar Of 365 Favorite Scriptures On Faith.* You want to begin a memorization program of one Scripture each day... your passion, *Faith.* It is important to tie together the focus of your life, *Faith*, with your daily living and circumstances. This calendar is a legacy for your family. Discuss your Scripture-of-the-Day on *Faith* at the breakfast table. Place it on your refrigerator door. Pin it on the bulletin board. I promise you, if you memorize 365 Scriptures on *Faith*, you will become the expert in *any* conversation!

3. *Collect Books And Tapes From Teachers Who Teach On Faith.* You will be amazed how the

Holy Spirit supernaturally guides your life into uncommon relationships with mentors to teach you.

4. *Keep A List Of Questions Regarding Faith.* This enables you to benefit from any moment you are in the presence of someone else who is an authority on *Faith.*

5. *Conclude Every Telephone Conversation With A Special Prayer For Your Friend That God Will "Increase Your Faith."*

6. *Listen To The Bible Daily On Cassette Tape. It increases your Faith.* "So then faith cometh by hearing, and hearing by the word of God" (Romans 10:17).

7. *Pray For Increased Understanding And Revelation Concerning Faith.* As you get alone with the Holy Spirit in the Secret Place, He will open your eyes of understanding. "Ask, and it shall be given you; seek, and ye shall find; knock, and it shall be opened unto you: for everyone that asketh receiveth; and he that seeketh findeth; and to him that knocketh it shall be opened" (Matthew 7:7,8).

8. *Set Aside A Specific Time Every Day To Read A Book On Faith.* Be militant and decisive about this appointment with Wisdom.

9. *Become Known For Your Obsession To Understand Faith.* When someone mentions Thomas Edison, everyone thinks about inventions. When someone mentions the Wright Brothers, everyone thinks of airplanes. It should be this way with you. Everyone should know about your passion—*Faith.* Open your church service quoting a verse concerning *Faith.*

10. *Maintain Your Wisdom Notebook On Faith.* Write down every thought, idea, and even poems on

Faith. You will be thrilled to see your progress in the coming 12 months. Your life and ministry should become remembered by this focus.

Whatever topic the Holy Spirit leads you toward, give it your total focus.

It will change your ministry forever.

Four Benefits Emerge When You Become An Expert On One Topic:

1. *Your Confidence Toward God Will Multiply.* His Word throbs with strength, energy and joy. Every word He speaks will breathe a new energy into your ministry unparalleled by anything else you do.

2. *Your Confidence Toward Your Own Dreams And Goals Will Increase.* Knowledge makes you comfortable. Knowledge increases your confidence about everything you do.

3. *Others Will Receive Your Ministry With Increased Confidence.* As your loved ones listen to the Word of God pouring from your lips, they will become excited about your ability to help them and increase their knowledge of God.

4. *Your Knowledge Of Other Subjects Will Instantly Increase.* For example, when you study angels, you will discover Lucifer and demon spirits, ex-angels de-throned by God. When you study Faith, you will learn so much about prayer, the Secret Place and the intercession ministry name of Jesus. When you study the Holy Spirit, you will fall in love with Jesus more than ever.

Master One Topic In The Bible.

It is one of the Secrets of The Uncommon Minister.

◈ 2 ◈

TREASURE THE CALL TO PREACH.

————◆————

You are more than a spiritual administrator.
You are more than the CEO of a church.
You are more than a counselor.
Your Assignment from God is to preach.
Preach until chains fall off the captives.
Preach until disease is destroyed.
Preach until the power of God falls.

Paul embraced his calling to preach, "Whereunto I am appointed a preacher, and an apostle, and a teacher of the Gentiles" (2 Timothy 1:11).

11 Facts About Preaching

1. *Preaching Is How God Manifests His Word.* "But hath in due times manifested His word through preaching, which is committed unto me..." (Titus 1:3).

2. *Preach To Persuade.* "Holding fast the faithful word as he hath been taught, that he may be able by sound doctrine both to exhort and to convince the gainsayers" (Titus 1:9).

3. *Preach To Protect Men From The Judgments And Wrath Of A Holy God.* "Knowing therefore the terror of the Lord, we persuade men" (2 Corinthians 5:11).

4.   *Preach Because It Is The Powerful Weapon That Saves People From Eternal Damnation.* "For the preaching of the cross is to them that perish foolishness; but unto us which are saved it is the power of God" (1 Corinthians 1:18).

5.   *Preach The Gospel Rather Than Your Personal Prejudices And Opinions.* "For Christ sent me not to baptize, but to preach the gospel: not with wisdom of words, less the cross of Christ should be made of none effect" (1 Corinthians 1:17).

6.   *Separate Yourself From Anything That Weakens The Effectiveness Of Your Preaching.* "Paul, a servant of Jesus Christ, called to be an apostle, separated unto the gospel of God" (Romans 1:1).

7.   *Preach Because You Are Accountable To God For The Souls Of Men And Women.* "Let a man so account of us, as of the ministers of Christ, and stewards of the mysteries of God. Moreover it is required in stewards, that a man be found faithful... but He that judgest me is the Lord" (1 Corinthians 4:1-4).

8.   *Preach To Birth Spiritual Sons And Daughters Under Your Anointing Who Will Carry On The Message After Your Passing.* "I write not these things to shame you, but as my beloved sons, I warn you. For though you have ten thousand instructors in Christ, yet, have ye not many fathers: for in Christ Jesus I have begotten you through the gospel" (1 Corinthians 4:14,15).

9.   *Preach To Inspire Others To Follow Your Pattern In Life.* The Apostle Paul understood this. "Wherefore I beseech you, be ye followers of me" (1 Corinthians 4:16).

10. *Preach More Strongly To Those Who Are Mature Enough To Receive It.* The Apostle Paul did. "But strong meat belongeth to them that are of full age, even those who by reason of use have their senses exercised to discern both good and evil" (Hebrews 5:14).

11. *Preach With Gratitude Because You Have Been Chosen By God Himself To Preach This Gospel.* The Apostle Paul lived thankful. "But the Lord said unto him, Go thy way: for he is a chosen vessel unto Me, to bear My name before the Gentiles, and kings, and the children of Israel" (Acts 9:15).

Treasure The Call To Preach.

It is one of the Secrets of The Uncommon Minister.

❧ 3 ❧

KNOW YOURSELF.

———————➤●◀———————

Study yourself.

Know Your Greatest Strength. One of my favorite people, Marilyn Hickey, shared an interesting illustration a few days ago when I spoke for her conference in Denver, Colorado. She had visited China. Admiring their World Class ping pong team, she asked the teachers how they corrected the weaknesses of their players. The reply came, "We ignore the weaknesses and focus on developing their strengths. Their strengths will override those weaknesses." This is a secret of Uncommon Champions.

Don't waste your entire ministry grieving over your weaknesses or failures. Find your *dominant* strength. Is it compassion for people? Is it long and enduring patience? Is it uncommon energy and enthusiasm? Is it the ability to be loyal in the face of adversity? Is it exceptional skill at management and administration? Is your speaking powerful, expressive or magnetic? Do you have the ability to *motivate* a small team around you? Is your greatest gift to hire uncommon staff? Your greatest strength is the Golden Gate to an *Uncommon* Ministry.

Know Your Greatest Weakness. Jesus knew the weakness of Peter, "Satan hath desired to have you, that he may sift you as wheat: But I have prayed for thee, that you faith fail not" (Luke 22:31,32).

I will never forget the shocking statement made by a famous and well-known pastor of our day. "My greatest weakness is women. Some men have a weakness for drugs, alcohol or gambling. I love beautiful women. So, I refuse to permit myself to be alone when I travel. I keep two businessmen with me every hour of the day." That seems absurd to a young novice in the ministry who believes that the power of God conquers all. But, the Uncommon Man of God refuses to "give place to the devil." He moves *away* from the temptation zone, not *toward* it.

Know Your Greatest Fear. Everything you do is moving you toward something you truly desire or away from something you fear. *Your fears are determining the kinds of decisions you make.*

Yesterday, a young man sat in the Wisdom Room of my home. He is a very effective and skilled young pastor from a distant city and state. He asked my counsel regarding a loan of almost two million dollars.

"Run from debt," I implored. "Give God time to produce a financial miracle. You see, debt will wipe the smile off your face. Debt changes the kinds of decisions you make. Debt will become your obsession, and you will lose the spontaneity and joy of your incredible ministry. Don't put your small congregation under that huge indebtedness. They will feel differently toward you than they do today. You will not feel it your first six or twelve months. But, the time will come when you will dread seeing that 20-year note every day."

After he left, several truths dawned. Apparently, he has no memories of really painful financial losses. He was new at pastoring. He saw only victories and joys ahead. I was speaking from my own past pain, fears and torments. I hate poverty.

I hate debt. I hate pain. I despise walking into a bank and having them respond to me like I have leprosy.

Know Your Own Needs. I need times of *solitude*. I need *changes*. I require great freedom of movement in my life. I love *order* around me. I enjoy candles, waterfalls, and water fountains. Climate matters to me. Because I recognize my needs, I can create the appropriate environment which unlocks my creativity and accommodates my needs.

Twenty years ago, I did not discern my own needs. Following a divorce, someone asked me, "What kind of furniture do you like?" I had no idea.

"Where would you like to live?" I'd never thought about it.

"What is your greatest goal of your life?" I could not really define it.

What do you need to keep *spiritually* motivated? What do you need and require from your closest friends? What do you require from your staff? What do you need financially to live the lifestyle you really enjoy?

I become amused at those who think I should "go hunting." I love animals. I have numerous animals and cannot imagine myself killing animals. You see, that's something my friends love to do.

Others insist that I "golf." I attempted it twice. For the life of me, I cannot imagine hitting a ball far away from me, going to where the ball landed and hitting it *further* away! Those who enjoy golf mystify me. It certainly is not exercise. Nobody walks fast. In fact, they use little golf carts! *Whatever.* Their needs are simply different than my own.

Know Yourself.

It is one of the Secrets of The Uncommon Minister.

☞ 4 ☜

ALWAYS ALLOW OTHERS ROOM TO TURN AROUND.

Everybody makes mistakes.

Everybody deserves the chance to change.

Permit them to do so.

When pressure increases, those around us are often affected. Their stress then influences us. The incessant, constant demands of others often birth impatience...and mistakes. During these moments, *your mercy is necessary.*

Wrong words are often blurted out.

Inaccurate assessments are made.

Wrong decisions occur.

Think back upon your own life. Many factors drove you to that moment of indiscretion, cutting words and angry outburst.

Permit forgiveness. *Do not force others to live by bad decisions in their past.* What you sow will come back to you a hundred times. Give them space to re-enter the relationship *with dignity.* "Blessed are the merciful, for they shall obtain mercy" (Matthew 5:7).

Forgive 490 times. "Then came Peter to Him, and said, Lord, how oft shall my brother sin against me, and I forgive him? till seven times? Jesus saith unto him, I say not unto thee, Until seven times:

but, Until seventy times seven." (Matthew 18:21,22). Forgive 70 times seven. Give them enough time. Things are happening which you cannot see. Sometimes it takes several weeks for a person to make a change.

▶ Give them a Season of *Silence*.

▶ Give them an open door for *Expression*...a chance to explain themselves. They may *not* have the right words the *first time*. Be willing to *listen longer*.

▶ Give them time to evaluate every part of the puzzle. You are looking at one part. They are considering many things they've yet to discuss with you.

▶ Give them time to discover the truth *about you*. You already know you. They do not. They do not know all of your *flaws*. They do not know all of your *capabilities*. They do not understand your *memories*. Your pain. Your goals or dreams.

Always Allow Others Room to Turn Around.

It is one of the Secrets of The Uncommon Minister.

❧ 5 ❧

TASTE YOUR PRESENT; IT HAS TAKEN YOU A LIFETIME TO GET HERE.

Moments should be tasted.

Your day should be *savored*, not gulped down.

Your life is a special and glorious gift from your Creator. Don't rush through it. Stop long enough to drink deep from each day. View each day as a wonderful fountain. Stop. Stand still. Take a deep drink from the sweet waters of the *Present*. You see, Today is really the only place you will ever exist. When you arrive in your future, you will *rename it...Today.*

Yesterday is in the *tomb.*

Tomorrow is in the *womb.*

If you do not know how to enjoy the Today that exists, you probably will not enjoy any day in your future.

Happiness is a Now Place. It is not a future destination or place of arrival. "This is the day which the Lord hath made; we will rejoice and be glad in it" (Psalm 118:24).

Savor this moment because the future is not guaranteed. "Whereas ye know not what shall be on the morrow. For what is your life? It is even a vapour, that appeareth for a little time, and then vanisheth away" (James 4:14).

Don't over schedule today with tasks you can do with more excellence tomorrow.

Raise your present turf to its highest level of excellence.

Insist that every moment be a Moment of Excellence. "Whatever you do, do with all your heart." *Conversations* should be conducted at the highest level. *Exercise* should be done properly. *Planning* should be thorough, not hurried.

Hurried lives are not necessarily productive lives. Busyness is not always a forward movement. Activity is not necessarily progressive. I've been around people who "flurry." Their emotional energy is higher than anyone around them. Yet, nothing truly significant occurs.

Calm and gentle people are not necessarily unproductive. Some of the most extraordinary and uncommon achievers appear to be methodical, unhurried and thoughtful. Their *decisions* are significant. Their instructions are *clear* and defined. Precision marks *every* step.

Progress is the result of genuine enthusiasm, not unfocused energy. Remember the playground? Laughter, energy and enthusiasm abounded. Thirty minutes later, everybody was tired, worn out or wanted to "do something else."

My own life is quite busy. Yesterday, I finished a conference in Virginia and took a plane to Pittsburgh. Then, I changed planes to fly to Ohio. I dictated two chapters in a new book, reviewed 20 to 30 pages of faxes, wrote letters, and telephoned seven pastors and friends. Then, I spoke at a special banquet for a church where $200,000 was committed to a new house of the Lord. The pastor met me this morning, drove me to the airport where I continued to dictate en route. I *read* on the plane, *dozed* a bit, and came straight to the hotel upon arrival.

Yet, nothing is in a frenzy around me.

Let me explain. When I walked into my beautiful suite here in Tampa, Florida, I took my cassette recorder out of my briefcase. Praise music has filled this beautiful hotel suite. I began to praise and worship and thank God for a wonderful life He has given me. Then, I called room service to bring me my dinner meal extra early. Service will begin in three hours. While waiting for my meal, I went downstairs to receive a special package of a new book from my printer. I unpacked my luggage, and within moments my meal had arrived. The atmosphere in this hotel room is marvelous. The Holy Spirit is here in an incredible way. No, I am not lonely. *He is here.* He is my *focus.* My life and my joy. Millions are attempting to fill their life with activities, new friends and "things."

But, I refuse to race through life.

I will walk through the Garden of Life, not run.

I will smell the fragrance of His presence, drinking deep from the Fountain of Peace. Certainly, there are moments when speed must be doubled to complete a significant goal that aids others, but I will walk...*not race*...through life.

Drink Deeply From The Present Moment; It Took You A Long Time To Get Here.

Seven Helpful Hints

1. *Cancel Any Ministry Appointment That Creates Too Much Haste, Hurry And Flurry.* Space things out more. For example, I realized one morning when I awakened, that the day was going to be miserable if I rushed to get a haircut. So, I called and *rescheduled.* I breathed easier, increased the excellence of the *present* tasks I was doing, and enjoyed the day.

2. *When You Have Made An Appointment Unwisely, Give Others An Opportunity To Reschedule.* Many times, I've had people to thank me for rescheduling! Their own agenda was too full. Their sense of loyalty prevented them from asking me to make a change. Sometimes, changes are better for everybody involved! "The Lord is good unto them that wait for Him, to the soul that seeketh Him. It is good that a man should both hope and quietly wait for the salvation of the Lord" (Lamentations 3:25, 26).

Jesus never hurried.

3. *Don't Rush Your Judgments Of Others.* Good or bad. Someone who makes a bad first impression, may turn out to be an uncommon blessing to your life. It has been said that first impressions are lasting impressions. Of course, this is not true at all. If that were true, divorces would never occur!

4. *Slow Down Your Eating.* Eat slowly, tasting the wonderful provision of God. Don't hurry your eating. Doctors tell us that this is the *best* way to eat. This had been a challenge for me, personally.

I am normally a very fast eater. Eating has always been an interruption, not an event. However, as the Holy Spirit has been helping me, I have been making mealtime a wonderful time of meditation, review and *thankfulness.*

5. *Look For Things To Enjoy,* not endure. What you look for, you will eventually see.

6. *Look For Qualities You Love* In Others, not qualities that agitate you. Be thankful.

7. *Concentrate On The Tasks That Really Produce Results,* not how many things you can get done.

Moving decisively with purpose is the opposite of lethargy and indifference. When you see someone move deliberately, it is not with lack of energy, or caring. It is often the opposite.

Always give total attention to the task at hand. As the Apostle Paul said, "Brethren, I count not myself to have apprehended: but this one thing I do, forgetting those things which are behind, and reaching forth unto those things which are before" (Philippians 3:14).

Taste Your Present; It Has Taken You A Lifetime To Get Here.

It is one of the Secrets of The Uncommon Minister.

☞ 6 ☞

SIT AT THE FEET OF THE BEST.

———————◄►◄————————

Advisors are everywhere.

Recently, a young pastor was discussing his difficulties with me. His ministry seemed to be a collection of tragedies and disappointments.

"Who is your mentor?" I suddenly asked.

He stumbled around a bit. He seemed uneasy and uncomfortable. So, I persisted.

"Well, there is a preacher that I talk to occasionally in the next town," he answered.

"Is he truly successful?" I asked.

"No, not really. But, he is someone to talk to," was his defensive reply.

I insisted that he needed a *worthy* mentor. A *capable* mentor. Someone *knowledgeable*.

"Would you consider becoming my mentor?" he asked.

"I am not even a pastor! Besides I am too busy with my own Assignment of writing, speaking and traveling. You need to learn from someone who is the best at what they do—*pastoring*."

I connected him to two friends of mine who are very successful pastors.

It is not enough to receive advice.

It is not enough to have a mentor.

You must learn the best from the Best.

When you want to improve your game of Ping-Pong, you must play someone who is *better* than you.

When you want to increase your wisdom, you must sit at the feet of those who *know more* than you.

Yes, this can be intimidating and uncomfortable. But it is the Road to Greatness. It guarantees increase.

Most simply want someone who is accessible and *within reach.* When I hire an attorney, I do not want someone who is merely inexpensive or near my home. I want someone who truly cares, is proven themselves in court and is known for excellence.

Some attend a church because it is near their house. How ridiculous! That's like marrying a man because he lives closer to your house than others. It's like buying a car because it is at the nearest lot.

Invest the time necessary to search for those who have established a good reputation.

There are hair salons close to my house. But, I drive further to the young lady who is the best. She does it right. She listens to me. She is not merely accessible. *Those who pursue convenience will never taste the Grapes of Excellence.*

Those who are willing to inconvenience themselves in their pursuit of excellence will create the most fulfilling and uncommon life imagined.

Do not purchase clothes simply because they are "on sale." Purchase clothes that present you *properly*, make you feel wonderful, and cause you want to wear them *every day* of your life.

Learning from the best may require a lower salary at the beginning. You are in for the long-term *success*, not the short-term *salary*.

A pastor picked me up from the airport recently. He told me something interesting about his son. His son had accepted a job at a much lower salary with another pastor. The reason? That specific pastor was a superb mentor. His own success was remarkable. The young man had enough sense to accept a job with lower salary...*so that he could learn from the very best.*

Learning from the Best may necessitate a geographical change. You might have to travel to another state. *Do it, if that is what it takes.*

Remember the specific knowledge you are seeking. If you're sitting at the feet of a great electrician, he may know little about protocol. But, you are not there to learn about protocol. You are there to learn about your career in electricity.

You will not learn everything from one Mentor during your life. Don't attempt it. It is too much stress on them, too. You may be disappointed. God never intended for you to do so. Many mentors are necessary to make you successful, learned and skilled throughout life.

Sit At The Feet Of The Very Best.

It is one of the Secrets of The Uncommon Minister.

7

TEACH YOUR PEOPLE TO SOW WITH EXPECTATION OF A HARVEST.

You can only do what you know. Thousands have been taught that it is wrong to expect something in return when you give something to God. They feel that this is greed.

"When I give to God, I expect nothing in return!" is the prideful claim of many who have been taught this terrible error.

Do you *expect* a paycheck from your boss at the end of a work week? Of course, you do. Is this greed? Hardly.

Did you *expect* forgiveness when you confessed your sins to Christ? Of course, you did. Is this greed? Hardly.

Stripping expectation from your Seed is theft of the greatest pleasure God knows.

His greatest *pleasure* is to be *believed.*

His greatest *pain* is to be *doubted.* "Without faith, it is impossible to please Him. For he that cometh to God must believe that He is, and...*that He is a rewarder...*of them who diligently seek Him" (Hebrews 11:6).

Motive means "*reason* for doing something."

When someone on trial is accused of a murder,

prosecutors try to find the possible motive or reason, why he was motivated to do such a horrible thing.

God uses harvest as a motivation for sowing Seed. He expects you to be motivated by supply, the promise of provision. "Give and it shall be given back to you, good measure, pressed down and shaken together, running over shall men give to your bosom" (Luke 6:38). This is much more than a simple principle of mercy and forgiveness. This is The Principle of Harvest.

God offers *overflow* as a *reason* you should sow Seed. "Honour the Lord with thy substance, and with the firstfruits of all thine increase: So shall thy barns be filled with plenty, and thy presses shall burst out with new wine" (Proverbs 3:9,10). Notice that He paints the picture of *overflowing* barns to motivate us (give us a reason for) honoring Him.

God promised benefits to those who might be fearful of tithing. "Bring ye all the tithes into the storehouse, that there may be meat in Mine house, and prove Me now herewith, saith the Lord of hosts, if I will not open you the windows of heaven, and pour you out a blessing, that there shall not be room enough to receive it" (Malachi 3:10).

Scriptures paint Portraits of Prosperity to inspire acts of obedience. Read Deuteronomy 28:1-14. In these Scriptures God creates a list of the specific blessings that will occur if you obey Him. Why does He give us these Portraits of Prosperity? To inspire and give us a reason for obedience.

Peter needed this kind of encouragement just like you and I do today. He felt such emptiness as he related to Christ that he and the others had "given up everything."

Jesus promised a one hundredfold return. "Then Peter began to say unto Him, Lo, we have left all, and have followed Thee. And Jesus answered and said, Verily I say unto you, There is no man that hath left house, or brethren, or sisters, or father, or mother, or wife, or children, or lands, for My sake, and the gospel's, But he shall receive an hundredfold now in this time, houses, and brethren, and sisters, and mothers, and children, and lands, with persecutions; and in the world to come eternal life" (Mark 10:28-30).

Many people think it is evil to sow Seed for a desired harvest. Ridiculous! *Harvest is the reason for sowing!*

Giving is the *cure* for greed.

When you sow, you have just mastered greed.

Greed *hoards*.

Man *withholds*.

Satan *steals*.

The nature of God alone is *giving*. When you give, you have just revealed the nature of God is within you.

The only pleasure God receives is through acts of faith. I stress this again. His *only* need is to be believed. His *greatest* need is to be believed. "God is not a man that He should lie" (Numbers 23:19).

Suppose an unbeliever approaches you after church and says, "I want to give my heart to Christ, Pastor." Suppose the unbeliever then says, "Will you pray that God will give me peace and forgiveness for my confession?"

Imagine yourself replying with indignation, "Of course not! That's greedy. You want something back for giving your heart to Christ?" They would be shocked if you said that.

Your Heavenly Father offers Supply for Seed; Forgiveness for Confession; Order for Chaos.

When Jesus talked to the woman at the well of Samaria, He promised her water that she would never thirst again. Was He wrong to offer her something if she pursued Him? Of course not. That was the purpose of the portrait of water—to motivate her and *give her a reason for obeying Him.*

One day, my dear friend, Dwight Thompson, the powerful evangelist, told me a story about the papaya. Somebody counted 470 papaya Seeds in a single papaya. If that was consistent, one papaya Seed will produce a plant containing ten papayas. If each of the ten contained 470 Seeds, there would be 4,700 papaya Seeds on one plant.

Now, just suppose you replant those 4,700 Seeds to create 4,700 more plants. Do you know how much 5,000 plants containing 5,000 Seeds would be? *Twenty five million Seeds...on the second planting alone.* Yet, we are having difficulty over really believing in the hundredfold return. Why?

Millions must *unlearn* the poisonous and traitorous teaching that it is wrong to expect anything in return.

A businessman approached me. "I don't really believe Jesus really meant what He said about the hundredfold. We've misunderstood that."

"So, you intend to teach Jesus how to talk when you get to heaven?" I laughed.

If God will do it for a papaya...He will do it for you and me. We are His children, not merely fruit on a tree!

I believe one of the major reasons people do not experience a supernatural, abundant Harvest of

Finances is because they really do not expect Jesus to do what He said He would do.

Eight Facts You Should Teach Your People About Expectation

1. *Expectation Is The Current That Makes The Seed Work For You.* "But without faith it is impossible to please Him: for he that cometh to God must believe that He is, and that He is a rewarder of them that diligently seek Him" (Hebrews 11:6).

2. *Expect Protection As God Promised.* "And I will rebuke the devourer for your sakes, and he shall not destroy the fruits of your ground; neither shall your vine cast her fruit before the time in the field, saith the Lord of hosts" (Malachi 3:11).

3. *Expect Favor From A Boaz Close To You.* "Give, and it shall be given unto you; good measure, pressed down, and shaken together, and running over, shall men give into your bosom. For with the same measure that ye mete withal it shall be measured to you again" (Luke 6:38).

4. *Expect Financial Ideas And Wisdom.* "But thou shalt remember the Lord thy God: for it is He that giveth thee power to get wealth" (Deuteronomy 8:18).

5. *Expect Your Enemies To Be Confused And Flee Before You.* "The Lord shall cause thine enemies that rise up against thee to be smitten before thy face: they shall come out against thee one way, and flee before thee seven ways" (Deuteronomy 28:7).

6. *Expect God To Bless You For Every Act Of Obedience.* "And it shall come to pass, if thou shalt hearken diligently unto the voice of the Lord thy God, to observe and to do all His commandments which I

command thee this day, that the Lord thy God will set thee on high above all nations of the earth: And all these blessings shall come on thee, and overtake thee, if thou shalt hearken unto the voice of the Lord thy God" (Deuteronomy 28:1,2).

7. *Expectation Affects God.* When you sow with expectation, your Seed will stand before God as a testimony of your faith and confidence.

▶ Sow, expecting God to respond favorably to every act of confidence in Him.

▶ Sow, from every paycheck.

▶ Sow, expectantly, generously and faithfully.

8. *When You Start Looking And Expecting God To Fulfill His Promise, The Harvest You've Needed So Long Will Come More Quickly And Bountifully Than You've Ever Dreamed.*

Pray this simple prayer: "Father, teach us the Wonder of Expectation. Show me how it pleasures You to be believed. Hasten the Harvest as we depend on Your incredible integrity. Show me how to unlock the expectations of my people so they can taste the rewards of an Uncommon Harvest. In Jesus' name. Amen."

Teach Your People To Sow With Expectation Of A Harvest.

It is one of the Secrets of The Uncommon Minister.

Complete your personal library of
"The Uncommon Minister" Series. These first seven
volumes are a must for your ministry reading.
Practical and powerful, these Wisdom Keys will enhance
your ministry expression for years to come.

Item	Title	Qty	Price	Total
B107	Volume 1 - Powerful Principles For Hitting Your Target For Success In Ministry		$5.00	$
B108	Volume 2 - Wisdom Keys For A Ministry Of Excellence And Greatness		$5.00	$
B109	Volume 3 - Winning Principles For Achieving Greatness In Your Ministry		$5.00	$
B110	Volume 4 - Principles On The Path To A Victorious Ministry		$5.00	$
B111	Volume 5 - Sign Posts On The Road To Excellence In Ministry		$5.00	$
B112	Volume 6 - Powerful Steps To A More Powerful Ministry		$5.00	$
B113	Volume 7 - Steps To Achieving Your Goals In Your Ministry		$5.00	$
	All 7 Volumes of The Uncommon Minister		$25.00	$
SORRY NO C.O.D.'S	Add 10% For Shipping			$
	(Canada add 20% to retail cost and 20% shipping)			$
	Enclosed Is My Seed-Faith Gift For Your Ministry			$
	Total Amount Enclosed			$

Name |__|__|__|__|__|__|__|__|__|__|__|__|__|__|__|__|__|__|__|__|__|__|__|__|__|

Address |__|__|__|__|__|__|__|__|__|__|__|__|__|__|__|__|__|__|__|__|__|__|__|__|__|

City |__|__|__|__|__|__|__|__|__|__|__|__|__|__|__|__|__|__|__|__|__|__|__|__|__|

State |__|__|__|__|__|__|__|__|__|__|__|__|__|__|__|__|__|__|__|__|__|__|__|__|__|

Zip |__|__|__|__|__| Telephone |__|__|__|■|__|__|■|__|__|__|

❏ Check   ❏ Money Order
❏ Visa   ❏ Master Card   ❏ Amex

Signature _____

Exp. Date _____

Card No. |__|__|__|__|__|__|__|__|__|__|__|__|__|__|__|__|__|

Mail To:
MIKE MURDOCK
M I N I S T R I E S
P.O. Box 99
Dallas, TX 75221
940-464-3020

Powerful Wisdom Books From Dr. Mike Murdock!

You can increase your Wisdom Library by purchasing any one of these great titles by Mike Murdock. Scriptural, practical, readable. These books are life-changing!

 ## The Covenant Of 58 Blessings

Dr. Murdock shares the phenomenon of the 58 Blessings, his experiences, testimonials, and the words of God Himself concerning the 58 Blessings. Your life will never be the same.! (Paperback) (B47) 86 pages $8

 ## The Proverbs 31 Woman

God's ultimate woman is described in Proverbs 31. Dr. Murdock breaks it down to the pure revelation of these marvelous qualities. (Paperback) (B49) 68 pages $7

 ## Wisdom - God's Golden Key To Success

In this book, Dr. Mike Murdock shares his insight into the Wisdom of God that will remove the veil of ignorance and propel you into the abundant life. (Paperback) (B70) 67 pages $7

 ## Secrets Of The Richest Man Who Ever Lived

This teaching on the life of Solomon will bring you to a higher level of understanding in the secrets of uncommon wealth and success. God's best will soon be yours as you learn and put into practice these keys. (Paperback) (B99) 192 pages $10

Remember... God sent His Son, but He left His Book!